W9-DGF-030

tEChiES™

Jerry Yang
and David Filo

Jerry Yang and David Filo

{ Chief Yahoos of Yahoo! }

JOSEPHA SHERMAN

TWENTY-FIRST CENTURY BOOKS

BROOKFIELD, CONNECTICUT

Special thanks to Bradley Wellington for contributing "Tech Talk"

Design by Lynne Amft

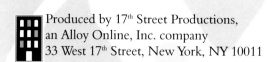

Produced by 17th Street Productions,
an Alloy Online, Inc. company
33 West 17th Street, New York, NY 10011

Library of Congress Cataloging-in-Publication Data
Sherman, Josepha.
   Jerry Yang and David Filo : chief yahoos of Yahoo! / by Josepha Sherman.
         p. cm. — (Techies)
   Includes index.
   ISBN 0-7613-1961-1 (lib. bdg.)
    1. Yang, Jerry—Juvenile literature. 2. Filo, David—Juvenile literature. 3. Electric
engineers—United States—Biography—Juvenile literature. 4. Yahoo! Inc.—Juvenile
literature. 5. Yahoo! (Computer file)—Juvenile literature. 6.Web search engines—Juvenile
literature. [1. Yang, Jerry. 2. Filo, David. 3. Businessmen. 4. Yahoo! Inc.] I. Title. II. Series.

TK 140.Y36.S54 2001
025.04'092'273—dc21
[B]
                                                                              00-066790

                    lib: 10 9 8 7 6 5 4 3 2 1

contents

CHAPTER ONE

Internet Innovators

From Worlds Apart

TAIPEI AND MOSS BLUFF DO NOT HAVE MUCH IN COMMON. TAIPEI IS THE CAPITAL OF TAIWAN AND ITS LARGEST CITY, AND MOSS BLUFF IS A SMALL TOWN IN SOUTHWEST LOUISIANA. BUT IN THE LATE 1960S BOTH TOWNS WERE THE BIRTHPLACES OF TWO BOYS WHO WOULD ORGANIZE THE INTERNET FOR THE WORLD. AT THAT TIME NO ONE HAD EVER EVEN HEARD OF THE TERM *SEARCH ENGINE*. A *YAHOO* WAS JUST SOMEONE WHO WAS NASTY AND LACKING IN GOOD MANNERS. THERE WAS NOT AN INTERNET. THERE WERE NOT EVEN ANY PERSONAL COMPUTERS!

Jerry Yang was born in 1968, in Taiwan, an island off the coast of China. His mother, a professor of language and drama, was Taiwanese, and his father came from mainland China. The happy new parents named their son Yang Chih-Yuan. In China the last name, or family name, comes first, so his personal name was Chih-Yuan. When Yang Chih-Yuan was

Chief Yahoo! Jerry Yang

only two, his father died. His mother was left to raise him and his year-old baby brother all by herself.

At first, Yang Chih-Yuan was too young to fully understand the challenges that came with his father's death. He was a bright, curious boy; as soon as he could talk, he began asking questions. Professor Yang says about her son: "Ever since he started to speak, he was always asking, 'What is this?' 'Why?' "

Yang's birthplace — Taipei, Taiwan

At age three the little boy began writing, of course in Chinese. He started wondering about the wider world around him. Yang Chih-Yuan certainly never guessed just how far from everything familiar he was going to travel.

Meanwhile, across the globe, another little boy was growing up in the town of Moss Bluff, Louisiana. David Filo was born in 1966, the second-youngest of six children. He was two years older than Yang Chi-Yuan, and he, too, was bright and curious. Of course he had no idea that a wild new world of computers and the Internet were waiting just a few years away. But like Yang Chi-Yuan, David Filo was already interested in all kinds of science.

Back in Taiwan, life was not easy for Yang Chih-Yuan's mother. Not only was she her children's only source of support, but there were not any jobs open to a woman professor. She realized that the only hope for her and her family was to leave Taiwan. When Yang Chi-Yuan was ten years old, he and his family immigrated to the United States. They settled in San Jose, California, where there were more jobs available to women, including ones for female professors.

Yang Chih-Yuan liked his new world. He wanted to fit in to it right away, so he decided that he wanted to change his name to sound more American. He followed the American custom of the family name following the personal name, picked an American first name, and became Jerry Yang. His younger brother became

The other Chief Yahoo!, David Filo

Ken Yang. His mother changed her name, too, to Lily Yang. She is now a professor of English and drama in San Jose.

Jerry Yang quickly learned to speak English. He also learned to read and write in English as quickly as he'd learned to read and write in Chinese. Yang was a straight-A student all the way through elementary school, high school, and college. In fact, he earned his bachelor's and master's degrees in electrical engineering at Stanford University in only four years, finishing his master of science degree in 1990.

But Yang wanted to go further with science. He continued to study at Stanford, aiming for a doctorate in electrical engineering. Meanwhile, David Filo had grown up and gone to college in New Orleans. He earned his bachelor's degree in computer

The city of New Orleans, where Filo attended Tulane University

engineering at Tulane University. He then decided to go to Stanford University; this is where he would meet Jerry Yang. Filo earned his master's degree in electrical engineering almost as quickly as Yang. Like Yang, Filo decided that he wanted to go on toward a doctorate in electrical engineering.

Stanford Years

It was in the doctoral program that Yang and Filo became good friends. They attended the same classes and studied the same subjects. More important, they shared an interest in computing and the new and rapidly growing Internet of the early 1990s. Filo found the Mosaic browser soon after it appeared on the Web, and he and Yang were hooked.

When Bill Gates had been in college, just a few years before Yang and Filo entered Stanford, he had already decided that he was going to start up the computer business that was to become Microsoft. But Yang and Filo had no intention of imitating Gates. In fact, they did not mean to start up a business at all. They both fully intended to stay at Stanford, finish their doctorates, and only then decide what they wanted to do.

But the Internet got in the way of their plans. So did some very dull courses. Filo says of his studies, which involved making tiny changes to plans for manufacturing computer chips, "I was terribly bored."

Yang agrees. "Really, we'd do anything to keep from working on our theses."

Together the young men began spending more and more time "surfing," or hunting through, the Internet and its newest creation, the World Wide Web. The World Wide Web, the familiar "www" in many Web site addresses, is the electronic network that links the wider electronic world of the Internet. Although of course it is not anything visible, it is named "the Web" after the intricate design of a spiderweb.

Surfing the Web

In the early 1990s it was not easy for people to find what they wanted on the Internet. There were literally hundreds of Web sites already out there, with more being added each day, and there was no simple way to locate anything. No one had yet come up with the idea of a "search engine," which is a computerized sorting system, a database that anyone surfing the

Stanford University, the original home of Yahoo.com

Internet can use for free to locate sites by subject.

Yang and Filo were not finding it easy to hunt down what they wanted on the Internet, either. Worse, when they finally did find a site they liked, they had no way of "bookmarking" it so that they could find it again.

"We'd wander around the Net," Filo says, "and find something interesting, and then I'd ask Jerry, 'Hey, where was that cool page we saw the other day,' and we could never remember where it was."

This, they decided jokingly, was a challenge worthy of their skills! It was also a really good way to avoid having to work on their graduate studies.

The Hot List

Yang and Filo set about making up their first computerized "hot list" of their favorite Web sites and categories, just for fun. The amount of information on the Web and the rate at which it was growing made it seem unmanageable, yet they had decided to do just that.

"David was great at it," Yang recalls. "He was really good at being able to consolidate that information."

Suddenly Yang and Filo realized the power of the Internet. The more networking there was of information, the more people used the Internet and the more powerful it became. It was an ever-growing process.

But they were not really planning to do anything important about it. Their list, they told each other, would be really handy when they wanted to find something on the Net again. Either of them would be able to "jump" directly to a site by clicking on its address in the list with the left button of his computer's mouse.

Some of Yang's friends in Stanford's engineering department heard about the list. It sounded really cool to them, and they wanted to use it, too. So as a favor to his friends, Yang put up the list on his computer workstation at Stanford University, using HTTP format. HTTP is a form of computer code, the computer language that gives the computer instructions. HTTP is called a *hypertext link* format. It allowed Internet users to log on to Yang's personal Web page, the Web site he had built for himself. From there they could click on a "link" on the page, which was a highlighted name or Web address, that would take them straight to whatever site they wanted.

While all this list searching was going on, Yang and Filo still had only their two Stanford University computer workstations available to them. The young men's first unofficial headquarters was a trailer on the grounds of Stanford University. The data for Yang and Filo's list were stored on Yang's computer, which he nicknamed Akebono. The search engine part of the list was stored on Filo's computer,

Sumo wrestler Akebono, the namesake of Yang's computer

which was nicknamed Konishiki. Yang was—and still is—an avid fan of the Japanese sport of sumo wrestling. He named their computers after two Hawaiian sumo wrestlers.

Now that the computers were named, what were Yang and Filo going to name their list? Neither of them could think of anything outstanding, so the first version of their database was simply called Jerry's Guide to the World Wide Web. But Yang did not want to leave Filo out since the database was partly his, too. He updated the name to Jerry and David's Guide to the World Wide Web.

Not the most catchy name, but what difference did that make? Yang and Filo did not think that the project was going anywhere. After all, it was meant just for themselves and a few friends.

But friends have friends. More and more people, both on the college campus and from outside, found out about the guide and started asking to use it. This meant redesigning their list for a wider audience. Yang and Filo worked to accommodate their audience, using special computer software, which is the series of codes, or instructions, that tells computers what to do. Soon people could access the database from off-campus computers as well.

By 1994 the once-simple database was getting pretty complicated. Yang and Filo gave up the idea of running their database from their computers alone and put the whole thing out onto the Web. Enthralled by the task they had undertaken, they still were not planning to make any money from it. They saw what they were doing as a favor to other Web surfers.

As their audience continued to grow, Yang and Filo continued to play with their guide, improving it and making it fancier. They added special features such as "Hard to Believe" for weird Web sites and "Cool Links" for sites they thought were really good.

"In the end," Yang says, "it was . . . the Internet, and its ability to influence tens of millions of people very rapidly, that got us really, really jazzed about doing what we were doing."

The fact that they were living off a grant helped, too—each of them had about $19,000 a year. Since the two doctoral students' only responsibility was to work on their dissertations, they could afford to "waste time" on their list.

Yang suspects that if he and Filo had been working on anything limited, like a magazine or newspaper, they would probably have gotten bored or tired and quit. But with anything as alive as the Internet, as soon as they posted an update online, somebody somewhere would promptly click on it. This proved to be a never-ending challenge! Yang and Filo would get so tired working on their list that they would want to stop, to get some sleep, but knowing that people they did not know were constantly using their list kept them working.

"And then a funny thing happened," Yang says.

The popularity of the list exploded. Yang and Filo hadn't stopped to think about just how many frustrated computer users there were in the world. The two young men were astonished to see their index quickly become one of the most popular sites on the Internet—and not just with local computer users. Their Internet index was now being used by people from all around the world!

This international usage kept right on happening, day after day. Without Yang or Filo advertising their list at all, the number of online visitors accessing their database doubled in the first month after they had posted it to the Web. And the number continued to double in every following month.

The faculty of Stanford University were not so happy about this sudden popularity. Too many people were using the Stanford computer network, and too many people were accessing Yang and Filo's index. The Stanford faculty could not get onto their own network.

"They told us we were crashing their system," Yang says, "and that we'd have to move the thing off campus."

This was quite an eye-opener for Yang and Filo. For the first time they realized that the whole thing had gotten much bigger than just two bored students' way to avoid studying. They had, to their amazement, stumbled into their own new computer business.

CHAPTER TWO

What's a Yahoo?

A Big Decision

JERRY YANG AND DAVID FILO WERE WELL AWARE OF HOW QUICKLY THE COMPUTER WORLD WAS GROWING AND EXPANDING. NEW BUSINESSES WERE STARTING UP EVERY DAY. MOST WERE FAILING JUST AS QUICKLY—BUT SOME WERE SUCCEEDING AMAZINGLY WELL. THEY DID NOT DARE WAIT. SO MANY PEOPLE WERE EXPERIMENTING WITH THE INTERNET THAT SOMEONE ELSE WAS SURE TO COME UP WITH A SIMILAR IDEA.

THE DECISION WAS MADE. YANG AND FILO TOOK LEAVES OF ABSENCE FROM STANFORD UNIVERSITY, PLANNING TO return someday and leaving their doctoral theses unfinished. Those theses remain unfinished to this day. That still bothers Yang. He says, "It was really, really hard to leave the Ph.D. program. I'm not a quitter."

But he knows that if he had stayed to finish his thesis, Yahoo! might never have been launched. Maybe a hundred people would have read his thesis, and of those, maybe five would have understood it.

"The attraction to Yahoo!," Yang adds, "was that millions of people were going to read what we produced."

As soon as Yang and Filo were gone, the faculty at Stanford University reclaimed their computer network, probably with sighs of relief. They were finally free to use the network to teach students such as Ken Yang, Jerry Yang's younger brother, who was now attending Stanford.

But what did Yang and Filo, the two new business partners, do next? Since they were still feeling their way along, they decided that a genuine business plan seemed the best way to go. As it happened, Yang had a friend, Tim Brady, who was attending Harvard University's business school. As one of his projects, Brady had to create a business plan. This was perfect for everyone. Brady got his project done using a real-life example, and Yang and Filo got a genuine business plan for free.

Actually, they never did use the plan that Brady created. Still, going over it did give Yang and Filo a chance to organize and focus their thoughts and to decide what, exactly, they wanted to do. There were dozens of ways to get onto the Internet, usually through tiny companies operating out of basements or garages. Most of these Internet service providers, or ISPs, as they are usually called, disappeared almost as quickly as they sprang up. But Yang and Filo had heard about a new company called Netscape Communications, which was going to release a product called Navigator. Navigator was a browser, a program to help people get to the Internet. Netscape Communications was far from being a tiny start-up doomed to fail overnight; it had already found funding. If Yang and Filo were going to start up a real business, they were going to need money, too. That meant that sooner or later they were going to have to convince someone to invest in their company.

After exploring their options, Yang and Filo were not sure in what direction they wanted to take their business. They did not even have a name for it. Yang and Filo worked late night after night, writing their own business plans for Internet-based companies and eventually rejecting plan after plan. They designed Internet shopping malls, then changed their minds. They even came up with the idea for an online bookseller, then dropped that, too—even as Jeff Bezos, founder of Amazon.com, was coming up with the same idea and turning it into a success. In between all their brainstorming they updated their online list.

Finally Yang and Filo realized that they had been right with their original idea. If they stopped their online list, they would lose all those people who were using it, and then they would not have anything. They were offering a service that people really wanted.

They already *had* the right business.

The Name Game

Now they just needed a name. Sometime back in early 1994—neither Yang nor Filo can remember the exact date—at about 2 A.M., after much thinking and feasting on junk food, they came up with the name Yahoo!, or, more officially, www.Yahoo.com.

Why Yahoo? Yang and Filo had already decided that their business should start with the words *Yet another* since there were so many new Net companies starting up. Yahoo! stands for "Yet Another Hierarchical Officious Oracle!" The *.com* (pronounced dot com) is the ending to a Web address that tells a computer how to find a site.

There were two other meanings to their choice: *Yahoo!* is a yell of excitement or victory. The other definition of *yahoo* is someone who is rough and unmannered. Yang won't say which definition he had at the back of his mind.

Yang and Filo quickly registered their address, www.Yahoo.com, so that no one else could use it. Yang and Filo crowned themselves Chief Yahoos. That's still the title they use. It even appears on Jerry's business card: "Jerry Yang: Chief Yahoo!," though now he has softened that a little by adding "Director" after it. David Filo's business card reads, "David Filo: Chief Yahoo!" with "Cofounder" under it.

Netscape offices in Mountain View, California

But what good was a company without a home? Since their directory had been exiled by Stanford University, Yang and Filo had to quickly find a new host, a computer site, for Yahoo!, or their new business was never going to survive.

During their frantic hunt Yang and Filo found a friend in Marc Andreessen. He is the cofounder of Netscape Communications, based in Mountain View, California. Netscape was quickly becoming one of the two big Internet browsers; Microsoft's Internet Explorer was the other. Andreessen agreed to let Netscape host Yahoo! and even loaned Yang and Filo computer workstations and other equipment, including phone lines.

Now their new business had an official name and an official online home. As soon as Yahoo! was up and running again, it continued to grow.

But how did Yahoo! actually work? One of the reasons for its popularity was that it was very easy to use:

Step 1: Go to the Yahoo! Web site at http://www.Yahoo.com, which is the complete URL, the computer version of a street address.

Step 2: Type a keyword into the query box. A keyword in a computer search is a basic subject word, such as *geology* or *Microsoft*, or a basic name such as *Bill Gates*, or even more than one word, such as *children's nonfiction books*.

Step 3: Click on the search button or the enter key.

Yahoo!'s computer programs then hunt through its database and other search engines, looking for the keyword in appropriate URLs, Web page titles, and texts. The results appear on the screen, listed and ranked in order of importance.

By November 1994 an amazing 170,000 people a day were using Yahoo!, and more were logging on with every new day. But Yang and Filo could not expand their company without money. They still had to find someone who would be willing to invest in their new company.

From Students to Businessmen

They found an investor in the same way that they found themselves owning a business—by doing something else. In this case, it happened during the search for a host for Yahoo!. Yang and Filo ran into Randy Adams, who operates the Internet Shopping Network. In early 1995 he was also just getting his business started. Adams introduced Yang and Filo to Mike Moritz, who was the head of an investment company called Sequoia Capital.

Moritz and the other members of Sequoia Capital instantly liked the idea of Yahoo!. As Moritz jokes about it, "It was a suicide impulse on our part" because any new Internet company was a risky investment. Most of them failed within a year.

But Moritz was used to taking risks and backing computer companies. He had already helped out Apple Computer and the software company Oracle, both of which became highly successful businesses. After meeting with Yang and Filo and liking what he had seen and heard, Moritz agreed to give the two young men a million dollars in exchange for a part interest in the new company. He also sent his businesspeople to help Yang and Filo fend off the sudden swarm of would-be buyers.

Yang and Filo needed the help. They were finding it very difficult to make the transition from graduate students to businessmen. They had never done anything like this before, after all. Yang admits: "We didn't know the right protocols. We said things we weren't supposed to say." He adds: "America Online offered to buy us outright."

America Online, known as AOL, is a very powerful company and one of the main Internet service providers, or ISPs. AOL's powerful reputation and financial offer tempted Yang and Filo. If they took whatever AOL offered them, they would have money but be out of work even before they really began.

They wanted to keep their new business more than they wanted AOL's money. Yang and Filo said no. A story ran in the *San Francisco Chronicle* anyhow, predicting that America Online would still buy Yahoo!. But to this date, Yahoo! remains independent.

Now that Yang and Filo had decided not to sell, they faced practical issues: Yahoo! might have a Web site, but now it needed a physical office as well. Yang and Filo decided on an office in Santa Clara, California, not too far from Netscape's office in Mountain View, and started looking for employees.

As electrical engineers, they had little business experience. They had never done anything like this. Remembering the work that Tim Brady had done for them when he had designed their first business plan, Yang and Filo contacted him first.

"It seemed like a natural move," Yang said. "He had all these ideas about marketing our product, so we made him director of marketing."

Brady told them that they needed to hire someone to do publicity. By now Yahoo! was not the only Internet search engine, although it remained the most unusual. Other search engines were less complete. They might offer a user a simple list of possible sites. Yahoo! instead offered users a whole tree, or outline of the information on the Web. A user might start with arts and humanities, for instance, then narrow the search down to literature and from there down to science fiction, and so on.

It was this unusual aspect of Yahoo! that Brady wanted them to publicize. This sounded like a good idea to Yang and Filo. After some research and recommendations they chose the Niehaus Ryan Group to handle the publicity.

That turned out to be a good choice. The agency understood exactly what they wanted. Since those early days Niehaus Ryan has continued to help Yahoo! handle its publicity.

Realizing that Yahoo!'s real strength is both in its system of categories and in its whimsical look and feel, the people at Niehaus Ryan came up with the unusual "Do you Yahoo?" commercials on television. They featured such odd characters as a young punk-rocker hunting for a quilting group he could join and a man with a monkey looking for a woman with a parrot. There were also similar offbeat advertisements in magazines and on billboards. An advertisement in a June 2000 issue of a computer magazine was even more unusual, combining an ad for Yahoo! with an ad for Intel, the major maker of computer chips that actually power computers.

Yang and Filo also needed to hire employees with computer knowledge. They hired a fellow Stanford student, Srinija Srinivasan. She was an expert in artificial intelligence, which is the term for computer programs that seem able to think for themselves. Since her job is the "heart" of Yahoo!, organizing the many levels of the search engines and keeping them running, her business card reads: "Srinija Srinivasan: Ontological Yahoo!" An ontologist is someone who studies the nature of existence.

However, Yahoo! still needed an executive. Yang and Filo were well aware that they were not businesspeople. They needed to hire a president and CEO, a chief executive officer, someone who already knew the business world. This certainly was not going to be a fellow student from Stanford. They would have to find someone older, with more experience than they or their staff of twelve employees had. But Yang and Filo did not want a stodgy, "color-inside-the-lines" executive. They needed to find a Yahoo like themselves.

The man they found was named Tim Koogle—and *dull* was a word that did not describe him.

The Right Man for the Job

Timothy Andrew Koogle—or Tim, or T. K., as he prefers to be called—was born on July 5, 1951. When he first met Yang and Filo in July 1995, he had just turned forty-five. That made him the oldest member of Yahoo! by almost twenty years.

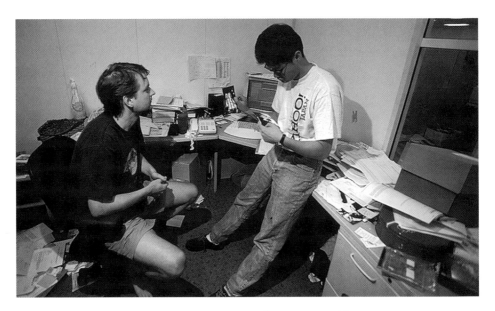

Yang and Filo keeping busy in the Yahoo! offices

Did the age difference bother him? Not really. Koogle could easily hold his own against any of the younger members of the Yahoo! staff, on several levels. He had graduated first in his class from the University of Virginia and, like Yang and Filo, had attended Stanford University for postgraduate study. Unlike Yang and Filo, he had actually graduated, earning a Ph.D. in engineering.

But there was another side to Koogle. During his free time in high school and college he had created and performed in two rock-and-roll bands, The Tides and Paraphernalia. Though neither exists anymore, Koogle still collects vintage electric and acoustic guitars, all of which he can play.

What is more, Koogle has some rather unusual skills for a businessman. He knows how to rebuild car engines, and he has done some fast-car driving as well. In fact, although Koogle had a full scholarship to Stanford, he lived off-campus and earned the rent by rebuilding the engines of other students' cars. Koogle was so successful at that side business, he actually bought a machine shop in which he worked in between going to classes.

"I love machines," Koogle says. "I'm fascinated by the way things move."

Yang and Filo thought that he would be perfect for a strange new computer company like Yahoo!, and they were right. At the time that Yang and Filo offered him a job, Koogle

Filo and Yang display the enormous fish prop used in a Yahoo! commercial.

was the president of Intermec, a manufacturer of data communications equipment. Before that he had worked for nine years at Motorola, Inc., in its financial department. He was ready for a new challenge.

He got one. When Koogle arrived at Yahoo! in July 1995, he was the only one wearing a suit. That did not bother him, and it did not bother Yang and Filo, either. Just because they preferred sneakers and T-shirts did not mean that their CEO must, too. Koogle continues to wear elegant black turtleneck sweaters and hand-painted ties—and Yang and Filo continue to wear their sneakers and T-shirts.

Karen Edwards, who is now Yahoo!'s director of marketing and brand management, says of Koogle: "Tim's always zooming in and out of cubicles with great enthusiasm and a great smile." She adds with her own smile, "He's cool."

When Koogle first arrived, he found a "very early stage company" that did not even have a logo. Yahoo! was just a second-floor office crowded with computer workstations, bicycles, games, and young people in jeans and T-shirts.

Yang's cubicle still has not changed much from the day when Koogle first saw it, with plastic milk crates for filing cabinets and magazines all over the floor.

Filo's office is not any more elegant. At any time a visitor might find a pile of dirty socks and T-shirts mixed in with books, papers, and software.

"I know we're not normal," Yang says with a laugh about their offices.

But aside from the clutter, Koogle liked what he saw: Yang and Filo were bright, determined young men who intended to succeed. "When I first met Jerry and David," he recalls, "what struck me immediately was that they had filled a fundamental need and they had done it intuitively." Koogle meant that the computing world had needed a search engine, and Yang and Filo had given them one without planning it out. "That's what you look for in starting a business." The next step was to organize.

CHAPTER THREE

Survival of the Fittest

Advertising Dollars

IT WAS GOOD TO OFFER YAHOO! TO INTERNET USERS AS A FREE SERVICE, KOOGLE TOLD YANG AND FILO, BUT A SUCCESSFUL BUSINESS HAD TO MAKE MONEY. AND MONEY COULD BE MADE THROUGH ADVERTISING.

AT FIRST YANG AND FILO DID NOT LIKE THE IDEA OF TURNING THEIR YAHOO! INTO A BUSINESS THAT RAN ADVERTISING. YANG POINTED OUT THAT THE PROGRAMS ON RADIO AND TELEVISION, EXCEPT FOR THE CABLE STATIONS, WERE BASICALLY FREE. KOOGLE COUNTERED THAT RADIO AND television were free exactly because they ran advertising to pay for the programs.

Yang and Filo could not argue with that. They let Koogle show them how they could keep Yahoo! as a free product and still make money. Yahoo! was founded in April 1994, but it opened officially on August 1, 1995.

Soon after the official opening, Yahoo! began selling advertising space. Most of these ads appeared on the top of each Yahoo! Web page. They were what are known as banner ads since they are long and narrow rectangles, like the shape of a banner. A curious Web surfer can click on a banner ad and be taken straight to the advertiser's Web site.

Yahoo! also features equally "clickable" ads on each subject page. These ads relate to the subject of the page. For instance, a page about literature might also carry a banner ad or a small, square side ad from an online bookseller. Yahoo! has a merchant partnership with companies such as Amazon.com, which means that they run ads on each other's sites.

Soon about four hundred companies were advertising on Yahoo!, lured by the idea that they could place their ads on pages that matched what they were selling.

Trouble in Paradise

Just as the company was taking off, a near disaster struck. Netscape Communications dropped Yahoo! and replaced it with another search engine. As the Web browser that had been hosting Yahoo!'s server, Netscape had also been listing it at the top of its directory page. When the owners of the new search engine offered Netscape a great deal of money for the space, Netscape replaced Yahoo!.

Potential investors in Yahoo! began to complain. They were sure that Yahoo! was going to be just another failed start-up Internet company. They were positive that the two young men from Stanford could never hold off competitors who had more money as well as the backing of big corporations.

Yang and Filo still had some supporters, though. Internet experts pointed out that the Web never would have been so popular without Yahoo!'s contributions. Without that search engine, users of Netscape's browser would have found little to browse.

Supporters and critics waited to see what Yang and Filo would do. Were they going to get angry? Would they make public attacks on Netscape? Or were they just going to surrender?

Yang and Filo, with the older, more businesswise Koogle to steady them, did not do any of that. Instead they kept up a calm relationship with the Netscape staff, working to get Netscape's management to reconsider. Surely it was not good business to link up with only one, top-bidding company.

"I'm pretty optimistic that we'll . . . work with Netscape again," Yang said. He added that he thought the whole Internet industry could well be hurt if Netscape's fees were too steep to allow search engines to make a profit.

But how would Yahoo! be affected? Yang and Filo must have been very nervous as they watched and waited. Would people still go to their site?

To their great relief, traffic on the Yahoo! site dipped only slightly, and only for a week. Then traffic came back up and, after that, rose to an even higher level than before. What had happened? Regular users of Yahoo! had already bookmarked the site. They found it again without needing to look for it on Netscape.

In early 1996, Netscape changed its policy. It announced that from now on, it would include several search engines in its list, each of which would pay Netscape the same set fee. Netscape agreed that it would no longer play favorites.

This development opened the way for Yahoo! to take a giant step forward. When a company starts becoming successful, there is a major way for it to remain financially safe: It can issue stock to the public.

Yahoo! Goes Public

When people buy a share of stock, that means they are buying a small piece of the company issuing the stock. They are gaining a small voice in that company. The more shares of a company's stock that a person owns, the more of a say that person may have. The money paid for the stock helps finance the company. The stockholder in turn gets a dividend every six months out of the company's profits.

On April 12, 1996, Yahoo! sold its first public stock. This first-time sale is called an IPO, or initial public offering. The opening price for Yahoo! stock was $13 a share. But people bought and bought. The closing price for Yahoo! stock that same day was $33 a share. This meant that Yahoo! had a stock market value of $848 million.

Yang and Filo were stunned. They finally had the funding to expand Yahoo! the way they had planned. They could go forward into new territory—technologically and geographically.

Before long Yahoo! was reaching into other countries, setting up branches of Yahoo! that focused on national tastes and wants as well as subjects. Soon Yahoo! Japan, for instance, was up and running, with listings that were specialized for Japan, and Yahoo! Canada was quickly doing the same thing for

Canada. There are also regional branches of Yahoo!, such as Yahoo! New York and Yahoo! Washington D.C. that offer surfers all types of local information, from restaurants to movies. The most recent additions to

On September 9, 1997, the trading begins for Yahoo! stock.

the international sites are Yahoo! China and Yahoo! en español, for Spanish-speaking surfers.

The More Things Change . . .

By 1997, Yahoo! had earned $67 million from advertising sales. Yang was listed on *Forbes* Technology's Richest list as number thirty-two out of two thousand. Neither Yang nor Filo wanted to spend all their new wealth. But Yang did buy himself a new car and a five-bedroom house overlooking San Francisco Bay for about $2 million. Filo kept his beat-up old car, not because he was being a miser but simply because he still liked it!

Even though they were both now wealthy, neither Yang nor Filo really wanted to upgrade their computer equipment. For one reason, they wanted to use what their customers were likely to be using. For another, it was inconvenient. When someone asked why Filo was working with an outdated machine, he just shrugged and said, "Upgrading is a pain."

In addition to their less than up-to-date computers, Yang still used an old 28.8 modem, the device that actually lets the computer access the Internet. The average speed of a modem in 1997 was 28.8 baud, which is a measurement of how quickly data can be transmitted. Even though there were faster modems, Yang wanted to be sure he knew what the average user of Yahoo! was experiencing.

But just because they were not buying the latest computer or modem upgrades did not mean that Yang and Filo were stingy. Now that they could afford charity on a large scale, they decided that it was time to make a donation to Stanford University. Maybe they felt grateful to the faculty for all they had learned while getting their master of science degrees there. Maybe they felt grateful to Stanford for letting them start Yahoo! there. Or maybe Yang and Filo felt a little guilty about having tied up the entire computer network for so long!

Whatever they might have been thinking, Yang and Filo gave Stanford University $2 million to endow a chair at the school of engineering. Yang added with a grin: "We hope the guy or woman who ends up taking the chair is also sort of a yahoo."

The Competition

In the first half of 1998 more than 30 million people a month visited Yahoo! and downloaded 100 million pages through that site every day. Yang was delighted by Yahoo!'s ever-growing popularity and welcomed everyone. Or almost everyone. In fact, about the only person Yang has said he ever wanted to

Onlookers watch the stock market react to Yahoo! earnings reports.

avoid, on or off Yahoo!, was Bill Gates, the founder and leader of Microsoft. Microsoft was so big and powerful a company that it alarmed Yang.

"You never, ever want to compete with Microsoft," he warned. "And even if they want to compete with you, you run away and do something else."

So far Microsoft has not really been in competition with Yahoo!. But that does not mean there have not been other competitors. There are anywhere from five to eight major search engines in any given year; the number changes every month or so, depending on which ones merge with others.

In 1998 a threatening challenger arose. The McKinley online directory tried to rival or outdo Yahoo! by adding reviews of Web sites to their search engine. These reviews looked so intriguing that Netscape Communications even invested in McKinley. Other investors, watching Netscape's actions, began to question if Yahoo! was such a good stock buy after all.

Yang quickly defended his company. He agreed that McKinley's reviews did look good. But were they really useful? Yang reminded everyone that the Internet changed so often that any reviews would be out-of-date even before they were posted. In fact, the sites that McKinley reviewed might have crashed or disappeared completely by the next day. Besides, with the literally hundreds of thousands of sites already on the Internet and the new ones being constantly added, how could any single company hope to post current and accurate reviews of them all?

This quickly proved to be the problem. McKinley's fame was short-lived. But another attack was soon mounted against Yahoo!, this time by Digital Equipment Corporation, DEC. DEC had created its own search engine, which was called Alta

Vista. The corporation advertised it as being the most powerful and accurate search engine on the Web. Behind this claim lay robotic computer systems, or "spiders," that attempted to index every scrap of information on the Web. This way, DEC claimed, users could search Web site contents as well as Web site titles.

Yang and Filo were not worried. They knew that the Web was, as Yang had already pointed out, constantly growing, too swiftly even for the swiftest and most complex of "spiders" to keep up. Sure enough, DEC officials soon had to admit that they were having problems with Alta Vista and with finding enough online storage space for all the data they were gathering. Alta Vista still exists, but in a less dramatic form. It is now linked with another search engine, Hotbot.com.

When Yang was asked whom he thought Yahoo!'s main competitors would be, he answered: "This space is changing constantly." He added that almost any organization with a strong online presence might turn into a competitor.

This was certainly true. The home page of any of the major search engines was no longer merely the place where someone could start a hunt on the Internet. Instead such a home page had become "feature rich," offering news, games, shopping, and other extras. It was now more properly called a Web portal.

One key difference between Yahoo! and other search engines—or Web portals—was that the Yahoo! listings were created by, as Yang said, "real people who surf the Web every day." He actually hired people whose jobs were simply to surf all day and bookmark what they found. Yang felt that this human touch put Yahoo! far ahead of rival search engines and their computerized "bots," or robot searchers.

Why didn't Yang and Filo link up with an ISP? They had already turned down that bid from America Online and hadn't accepted bids from any other ISPs afterward. It was still too soon to know whom Yahoo! wanted for a partner. "Who will be the big Internet access provider two years from now?" Yang asked. "It's just too early to tell," he added. "It'd be great if we could pick the winner. But we might pick the loser."

Yahoo! didn't really need to link up with an ISP, anyway. It was now earning more than $300,000 in advertising every month, with more than eighty major companies running ads on the site, from Bank of America to Honda.

As Chief Yahoos, Yang and Filo could have paid themselves high salaries. But they were content to pay themselves only $50,000 apiece per year, which is less than many employees earned.

A Hot Property

Now that Yahoo! seemed certain to survive, investors once again became very interested in it. With Koogle's help, Yang and Filo could be very selective about which investors they picked. They finally agreed to let a Japanese publishing corporation, Softbank, invest almost $64 million in Yahoo!. Softbank had already bought Ziff Davis Publications, which publishes several computer magazines and has its own computer-oriented Web site, www.Zdnet.com.

Softbank now owned nearly 23 percent of Yahoo!. In comparison, Yang and Filo each owned only about 8 or 9 percent apiece. Why did they decide on Softbank as such a large investor when they had turned down America Online?

"Our major partners are not Internet companies," Yang says. He did not want to merge with a possible competitor or with a company that wanted to buy Yahoo!. Yang and Filo were looking instead for outside companies that might be interested in the Internet and that would be willing to grow with Yahoo! rather than try to take it over.

In December 1998, *PC Magazine* named Jerry Yang and David Filo its People of the Year. Despite all challenges Yahoo! was still the most used and most successful of any of the Web portals. In fact, *PC Magazine* described it as "a full-featured one-stop Web service center that can occupy its visitors for an entire day."

Yang and Filo had come a long way from the days of Jerry and David's Guide to the World Wide Web.

Teamwork

In January 1999, Yang and Filo promoted another important member of the Yahoo! staff. His name was Jeff Mallett. He became Yahoo!'s chief operating officer, or COO. An operating officer is responsible for the actual workings of a company. Koogle, who was quite busy with the title of CEO, was happy to give up the title of president to Mallett.

True to Yahoo! form, Jeff Mallett was not a stodgy executive. Only a few years older than Yang and Filo, Mallett was every bit as unusual as any other Yahoo! employee. A Canadian citizen, he hadn't originally planned to go into the Internet business or, for that matter, into any traditional business at all. Mallett had fully intended to become a professional soccer player.

He was good enough to play professionally. While attending the University of Victoria on Vancouver Island in Canada, Mallett had actually been invited to sign with the North American Soccer League. But he was not sure that the NASL was going to survive, so he turned them down. Besides, at the time Mallett preferred to stay in Canada, even though all he could find there were amateur and semiprofessional teams.

Sure enough, just as Mallett had predicted, the North American Soccer League failed. There did not seem to be much of a chance for Mallett ever to play soccer on a professional level now. And he had gone as far as he could in the semiprofessional games. Mallett left the sport and began working with his father on a start-up electrical business. When they sold the company, Mallett used his share of the money to attend San Francisco State University.

But he was not a "traditional" student. He quickly grew bored with formal lessons. So Mallett started working with a professor on a business plan for a spell-checking and grammar-correcting software system. The company they formed was called Reference Software. In 1992 it was sold to WordPerfect, which in turn was bought by Novell.

Novell hired Mallett to work in its home office in Utah. He became vice president of the consumer division. But Mallett realized that he was not cut out to be a traditional executive, either. He soon found his job with Novell boring, too.

Then Mallett received a telephone call from Jerry Yang. Yahoo! flew him out to Santa Clara to meet with Yang and Koogle.

It was a great meeting. Mallett says: "I was just flat-out floored by these guys. I stayed up all night, called them the next day, and said, 'Yeah, I'll give it a swing.' And that was that."

How did someone with a software background wind up as a major executive of a new media company like Yahoo!? Mallett thinks it has to do with the fact that this was not a standard business situation. An airline company, for example, needs to know that the person they are hiring to fly an airplane is a qualified pilot for that specific type of plane. But when it came to working with the Internet, no one was completely certain yet what the Internet—and Yahoo!—could do or what skills an employee might need.

"We're very fortunate," Mallett says, "because T. K."—who is Tim Koogle—"Jerry"—who is Yang—"and myself, we're three amigos." In other words, the three men like one another and work well together.

Nuts and Bolts

What about David Filo? As usual, he was perfectly content to let Yang handle the business side of Yahoo!. He was too busy handling the technical side, keeping the "nuts and bolts" of Yahoo! updated and running smoothly. Filo says: "Yahoo! began life at Stanford University on a DEC Alpha box running OSF and a Sparc 20 running SunOs."

What that means is that Yang and Filo were using very basic computer workstations that were running rather primitive operating systems, at least by today's standards. The computers and operating systems were far too slow and simple to run Yahoo!'s now-very-complicated programs.

Filo was on a constant search for more stable and more efficient systems for Yahoo!. He tried several in the early days of Yahoo!, including programs from companies such as SGI and Linux. Linux is a big name in the computer world right now, since it may prove to be a genuine rival to Microsoft's Windows operating system. But it just was not right for what Filo wanted for Yahoo!. He finally found an operating system called FreeBSD.

At first Filo was skeptical about FreeBSD. He says: "Having spent many frustrating hours trying to install other PC OS's," which are computer operating systems, "I was a bit skeptical." Anyone who has ever had problems installing a computer operating system, or any other software, understands that view.

Although FreeBSD is a specialized program that is not commonly used by the public, it turned out to be exactly what

Filo needed—a stable and efficient operating system for a company as complicated as Yahoo!.

In 1999, Yang was listed as thirteenth on *Time Digital's* top-fifty list. At age thirty he was now worth about $3 billion. To his satisfaction, Yahoo! was still totally free to users. And Yahoo! was actually continuing to make money through advertising, which made it rare among Internet businesses. Jeff Bezos's online bookstore, Amazon.com, for instance, has been in business almost as long as Yahoo!. It is considered to be one of the top merchants on the Internet. But it has yet to show a profit. It is strange to think that Amazon.com first became popular through a listing in Yahoo!'s "What's Cool" section when Yahoo! was just getting started.

Today Yahoo! continues to grow. At the end of 1999 it acquired Geocities, which is an online community of loosely linked personal Web sites. It also acquired an online media company, Broadcast.com.

CHAPTER FOUR

Back to the Future

We're Number One

As of early 2000, Yahoo! had become a truly worldwide Internet communications network, a media and commerce company that offered its services to more than 120 million users around the world every month. An on-line business magazine, *The Standard*, announced that "Round One of the portal wars is over, and Yahoo! has won." Of the four main search engine Web portals, which in early 2000 were Excite, Infoseek, Lycos, and Yahoo!, Yahoo! had the highest income, the most users, and the best name recognition. It had become the number-one-visited site on the Internet.

Koogle agrees with Yang and Filo that Yahoo! should remain strictly a Web-based business. He does not think Yahoo! should try to own everything from Web sites to television stations. Instead Koogle intends to stick to offering surfers "a friendly gateway to the Web." He says: "Our core belief has always been: Put yourself in your users' shoes. Try to view the Internet through their eyes. Try to think about the easiest way of presenting them stuff that will be relevant to them."

This does not mean that Koogle wants Yahoo! to stagnate. He has overseen changes, such as the introduction of live broadcasts of financial tips, and plans further live broadcasts in the future.

"We anticipate stuff," Koogle states, "because we live this every day. And we've got a critical mass of very smart people here who also are pretty good at anticipating things over the horizon."

How do sites get listed on Yahoo!? Some sites are selected by Yang, Filo, or Koogle. Most, though, are found or checked out by other members of the staff, those people who were hired specifically to be surfers. Still other sites may be nominated by the owners of the sites themselves or by independent surfers who have found "a really cool site" they want to see listed on Yahoo!.

The listings of sites or Yahoo!s (as the Yahoo! home page spells it) are seemingly endless. In addition, there are also the numerous Yahoo! Guides, Yahoo! Entertainment, Yahoo! Publishing, and Yahoo! Small Business.

Another aspect of the site is Yahoo! Shopping, which is Yahoo!'s online shopping center. Yahoo! does not do the selling. Instead it provides virtual—as opposed to solid—storefronts for merchants and charges them "rent." Since there are not any real warehouses or workers, this arrangement makes money for everyone involved in the shopping center's stores. In 1999, Yahoo! added an online auction site, Yahoo! Auctions, to its online shopping experiences. In addition to the shopping center is a virtual post office—Yahoo! offers free e-mail at Yahoo! Mail.

Business users are not neglected, either. They can find a host for a virtual store and a source of animation or music for a Web site, as well as tools to design or improve that Web site. They can also check the local or national news and weather, get stock quotes, find an office space or an apartment, or work out a retirement plan. They can even stop for a quick game of online cards, join a club on one of dozens of subjects, page an acquaintance who is also online, or take in a live-time chat session.

Karen Edwards, Yahoo!'s brand marketing expert, has seen to it that Yahoo!, unlike the day when Tim Koogle first arrived there, now definitely has a logo. It can be seen on twenty different Yahoo! T-shirts and Yahoo! computer bags—as well as in a yearly floral display growing in Edwards's garden.

Expansion

Yahoo! is not limited to one physical office any longer, either. The headquarters is still in Santa Clara, but Yahoo! also has offices in Europe, Asia, the Pacific, Latin America, and Canada—as well as several in the United States. The staff that used to number only two now numbers about two thousand.

What is it like to work at Yahoo!? A new employee has to be prepared for everything from long hours of hard work to wild Frisbee matches. Edwards jokes that the new employees also have to be prepared to see a great deal of Yahoo!'s yellow and purple colors on chairs, sofas, and walls. Employees still like to work at Yahoo! in spite of all that yellow and purple!

Yang and Filo know that even with all the additions they've made to Yahoo!, they can't stop now. There were at least 115 million Web sites in 1999 and are probably twice that number by now. Yahoo! has to keep growing and changing with the World Wide Web.

As Yang puts it, "There's this huge, fast-moving train called the Internet. And we're just half a mile ahead laying the tracks to make sure it doesn't go off the cliff." He adds, "It's felt that way since the very beginning."

Meetings and Mergers

In March 2000 the train suddenly seemed to be picking up speed, nearly overtaking those laying the tracks. America Online made a bold move, catching almost everyone in the computer world off guard. AOL announced that it was going to merge with publishing and movie corporation Time-Warner.

How was this supermerger going to affect Yahoo!? Had Yang already been making merger plans of his own? Rumors were spreading that Yang and Filo were considering a partnership with publishing tycoon Rupert Murdoch, owner of HarperCollins, William Morrow, and several newspapers and television stations. A report published in *The New Yorker* magazine said that such a deal would give users access to Yahoo! through Murdoch's News Corporation's satellite systems. The report added that Yang had already met several times with the News Corporation's president, Peter Chernin.

Is the report accurate? Only Jerry Yang, David Filo, and Tim Koogle know for sure—and they are not telling.

In the meantime, though, the people of Yahoo! were working on some other plans. In July 2000, Yahoo! purchased its third company of the new year. This time it bought a software provider company called Encompass.

Encompass provides what is called connectivity software; that is, software to allow a customer to get connected to the Web in under five minutes. Some of Encompass's customers include Dell Computers, which is another very successful Internet business, and AT&T, which provides Internet access through its attglobal.net branch.

Does this mean that Yahoo! really is trying to rival America Online? Jeff Mallett insists that buying Encompass does not mean that Yahoo! wants to be an Internet service provider.

Instead, he says: "We're expanding our business services, which, two years ago, we didn't have."

Neither he nor Jerry Yang will talk more about that.

However, Yang likes to talk about almost everything else. He has become a genuine businessperson—and a little of a showperson as well.

It is fortunate that Yang likes to do publicity because David Filo, even today, remains the very opposite. Filo much prefers to stay behind the scenes, working on computers and computer programs. This sometimes means staying in the office all night. It can even mean sleeping there—at least if Filo's girlfriend is out of town.

But Jerry Yang does have a true talent for public relations. He is the one who grants newspaper and magazine interviews and who appears on television. He plainly enjoys it, too. Yang has delivered the keynote addresses at many major computer and business conventions, such as Internet World and COMDEX—which is a big, yearly exposition of new computer products—and *Fortune* and *Wall Street Journal*

TECH TALK

Search Engines

Anyone who has used a search engine knows that it is a tool used to find content on the Internet. How do these search engines work? Do they really know about every single Web page? How do they keep track of this vast amount of constantly changing information?

Let's walk through a simple example. When you go to a search engine and ask it to look for information about houses, what exactly does it do?

What the search engine appears to do is go through every page on the Internet and pick which ones match what you asked for. But if the search engine actually looked through every single Web page on the Internet, it would take far too long to be useful.

So if it doesn't look through the actual pages, how does it find what you want?

What a search engine does is gather special information about every Web page before it is ever asked anything. The information that is gathered is called meta-data. Meta-data is information about information. The page you're reading now is full of information, so what would its meta-data look like? Meta-data about this section could look like this:

Title: Search Engines
Subject: Search Engines
Keywords: Search Engine, Internet, Yahoo, meta-data

The advantage of using meta-data is that when you are looking for something there is much less information to look through to find it. Now the search engine can look through meta-data to find what you want. That is hundreds of times quicker then reading the whole page.

How do these search engines get all of this meta-data? A search engine uses what is called a Web crawler. A Web crawler is a computer program that is written to go out and gather information on various Web pages. You could think of the Web crawler as a person who is visiting Web pages and filling out index cards describing the content of each page. As a Web crawler sees a page, it will generate meta-data on the page and then report back to the search engine.

When you make your query, "houses," the search engine will send you all the information it has where the subject, title, or keyword is houses. All search engines keep meta-data a little differently, and that is why they will all give you back slightly different information.

A new venture for Yahoo! — laptop-equipped taxis with Internet access

conferences. He has been the feature subject in magazines from *Forbes* to *Newsweek* and has appeared on the covers of *Time* and *BusinessWeek* magazines. Yang is also a regular speaker on such business programs as CNN, C-SPAN, and Fox News.

In between his media appearances he is traveling the globe. He travels often enough that his staff cannot always say where he is. Yang is on the road at least two to three times a month. He jokes that he deals with jet lag by staying "really, really tired—that way I can sleep whenever, wherever."

Like other international travelers, Yang has discovered a few unexpected cultural problems. When he was in Japan, where people bow to show courtesy, he learned, too late, that he had been bowing not like a man, with hands to the sides, but like a woman, with hands in front of him! He has stumbled over foreign names before, too. Yang tries to learn the names of all the people with whom he is meeting—and to learn how to pronounce those names. He admits that he has not mastered this skill yet!

How does Yang keep in touch with his wife and with Yahoo! while traveling? By e-mail, of course.

# Big Issues

But not everything concerning Yahoo! is fun for Yang and Filo. Privacy is a big issue on the Internet nowadays. Yahoo! was criticized for collecting a good deal of personal information from its users. But Tim Koogle has gone on record, and so has Jerry Yang, stating firmly that they do not sell the information they gather.

"We're not going to be in the list-selling business," Koogle says, "or in the data-selling business."

Another serious matter came up in June 2000. The French judicial system noticed that a site advertising Nazi memorabilia for sale could be reached through the Yahoo! Web portal. It is illegal in France to sell any objects linked to racism. So the French government told Yang that Yahoo! had to block French Web surfers from the site.

Yang was outraged. He was certainly not about to promote racism, but he also was not about to censor Yahoo!—even if such a thing were possible. The Internet, after all, is not a solid object like a door that can be locked. Yang told the French newspaper *Libération*: "Asking us to filter access to our sites according to the nationality of Web surfers is very naive."

Free Time?

What, though, do Yang and Filo like to do in their time off? There is not that much time off. Yang likes golfing, though he admits he is not very good at it, and watching sumo wrestling. He is also very close to his his mother and brother—and adores his mother's cooking!

Filo, of course, likes to work with computers. He claims to sleep every third night. Filo likes to write, too, and has written a book called *Yahoo! Unplugged: Your Discovery Guide to the Web*, with contributions from the rest of the Yahoo! staff. Based on Yahoo! itself, the book is a guide to what Filo rates as the best sites on the Web.

Jerry Yang takes a lighter view. He sums the Yahoo! experience up for himself and David Filo as, "I'm having a great time. This is the best job I've ever had." But then he pauses. "Actually," Yang adds honestly, "it's the only job I've ever had."

Yet, in 2001, the technology market began to fade. Many of the "dot.com" companies lost a great deal of their stock value, and several shut down. Yahoo.com still exists, but it wasn't entirely safe from the upheavals. Tim Koogle stunned the online and financial worlds by resigning. Yahoo.com is still operating—and if Jerry Yang and David Filo have their way, they will be keeping their jobs as Chief Yahoos for a long time to come.

sources and bibliography

Filo, David and Jerry Yang, and others. *Yahoo! Unplugged: Your Discovery Guide to the Web.* Boston: IDG Books Worldwide, 1995.

The following online services were also used:

www.business2.com

www.businessweek.com

www.forbes.com

www.readersndex.com

www.tdo.com/local/graphics/1pyang/1pyang.htm

www.time.com

www.thestandard.com

www.yahoo.com

www.zdnet.com

index

Page numbers in *italics* refer to illustrations.

78

Photography credits

AP/Wide World Photos, 8, 11, 15, 18, 28, 36, 38, 47, 50, 72
PictureQuest, 9, 12